Amazing Planes

by Frances Ridley

ticktock

Contents

Words in **bold** are explained in the glossary.

Copyright © **ticktock Entertainment Ltd 2008**
First published in Great Britain in 2008 by **ticktock Media Ltd.**,
Unit 2, Orchard Business Centre, North Farm Road,
Tunbridge Wells, Kent, TN2 3XF

We would like to thank: Penny Worms, Alix Wood and the National Literacy Trust.

ISBN 978 1 84696 774 0

Printed in China

Picture credits: b=bottom; c=centre; t=top; r=right; l=left
Aviation Picture Library: 3, 6-7, 8-9c, 10-11, 12-13, 14-15, 16-17, back cover cr; Corbis: 2, 4-5, 9t, 20-21,
back cover cl; NASA: 18-19, 22-23.

Every effort has been made to trace the copyright holders, and we apologise in advance for any
unintentional omissions. We would be pleased to insert the appropriate acknowledgements
in any subsequent edition of this publication.

Airbus A380

The Airbus A380 is the largest airliner in the world. It has two engines on each wing. It carries 853 passengers.

The Airbus A380 has three decks. One deck is for **cargo**. The other two decks are for passengers.

4

There are shops and places to eat on the Airbus. There are children's play areas, too!

SR-71 Blackbird

The SR-71 Blackbird is a spy plane. It carries cameras and **sensors** for spying and spotting enemy planes.

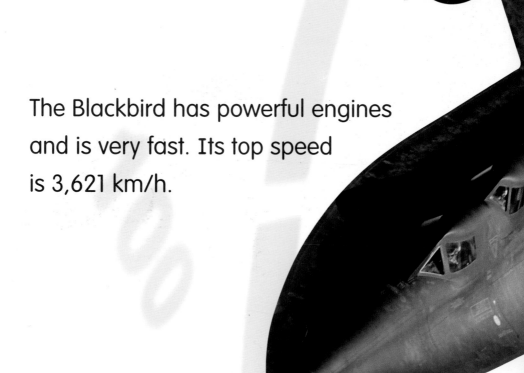

The Blackbird has powerful engines and is very fast. Its top speed is 3,621 km/h.

The plane is made from a
special metal. This keeps the
plane cool when it goes very fast.

Boeing 747

Boeing launched the 747 in 1966. It was the first passenger plane to have two aisles of seats. It was called the 'Jumbo Jet' because it was so big!

Modern
Boeing 747s
also carry
cargo. The
747-400F has a
nose that lifts up.
You load the cargo through the nose!

B-2 Spirit

The B-2 Spirit is a stealth aircraft, which means it's almost invisible to **radar**.

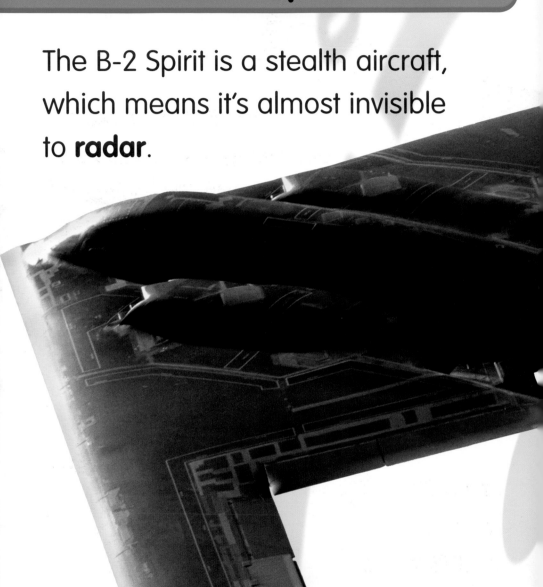

The B-2 looks like a giant wing. Its skin is black and smooth. The bulges hide the engines, cockpit and bombs.

The B-2's top speed is 1,013 km/h. It makes less noise than normal planes.

Eurofighter Typhoon

The Eurofighter Typhoon is a warplane. It carries a gun, missiles and bombs.

Most of the Typhoon's body is made of carbon fibre. Carbon fibre is light. It keeps the plane cool at high speeds.

The Typhoon's top speed is 2,129 km/h. It has two engines. It can take off in only five seconds!

F117A Nighthawk

The Nighthawk is a bomber.
Its top speed is 1,126 km/h.

The Nighthawk's strange shape
makes it hard to spot by radar.

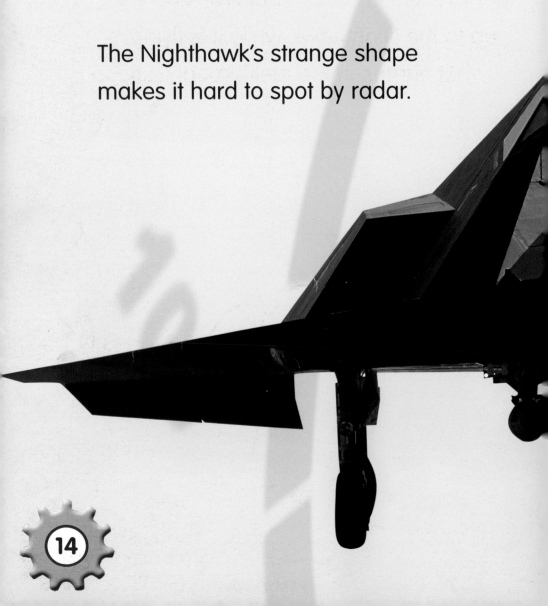

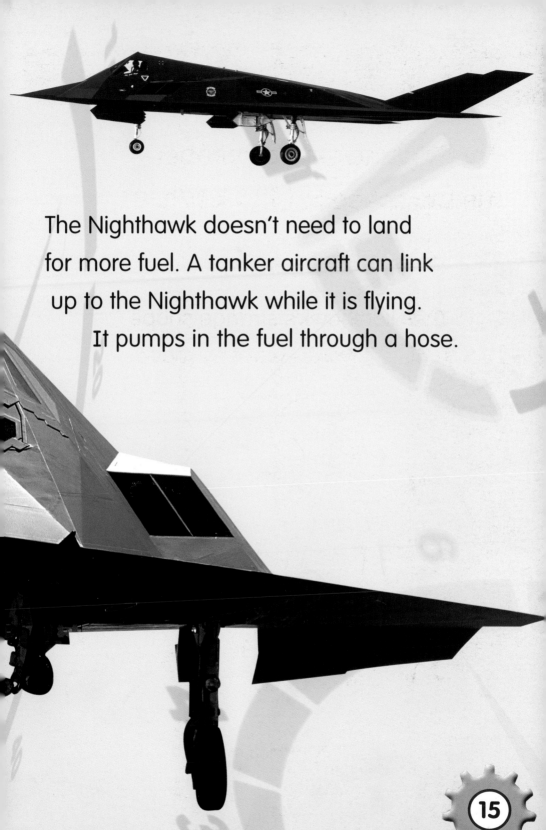

The Nighthawk doesn't need to land
for more fuel. A tanker aircraft can link
up to the Nighthawk while it is flying.
It pumps in the fuel through a hose.

Harrier Jump Jet

The Harrier was the first **VTOL** aircraft. A VTOL aircraft doesn't need a runway. It can take off and land from a ship, a forest clearing or a park!

The Harrier has a special design. It can change direction very fast. This makes it hard to follow and chase.

Space Shuttle

The Space Shuttle takes people and **satellites** to space. A huge fuel tank launches the Shuttle. Then it uses fuel from two rocket boosters. The rocket boosters fall off when they are empty.

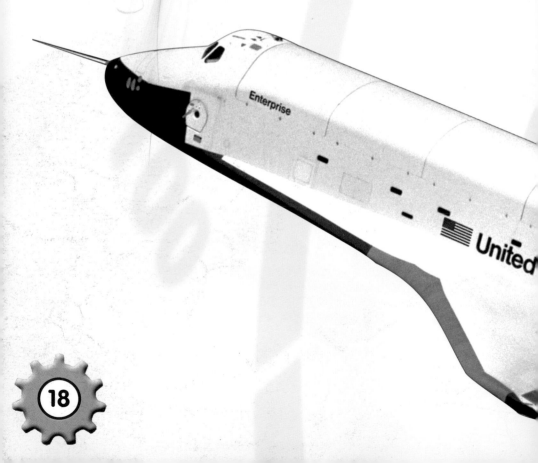

Special tiles help to keep
the Shuttle cool when it
comes back to Earth.
It lands on a runway.
A huge parachute
slows it down.

Voyager

In 1986, Voyager flew round the world non-stop. No plane had ever done this before.

Voyager looks very strange. Its body is fixed in the middle of two long wings. The body holds all the fuel it needs.

Two people were on board. They had to lie down to fly the plane!

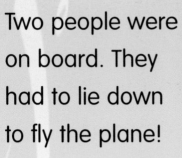

X43A

NASA is famous for making space rockets. It also carries out research into aircraft.

The X43A has no pilot. It goes too fast for humans to survive. Its top speed is 10,621 km/h!

The X43A is carried into the sky by a plane and then launched.

This is the X43A on the end of the Hyper-X rocket that launches it.

Glossary

cargo	Goods carried on planes.
radar	A way to detect objects far away.
satellites	A man-made object that is put into space to collect information.
sensors	Special equipment that helps pilots to fly planes, fire weapons and spot enemy planes.
VTOL	Stands for **V**ertical **T**ake-**O**ff and **L**anding. Planes that can lift into the air, without needing a runway.

Index